Contents

Introduction

Energy planning

Before contemplating measures to enhance the thermal performance of a historic building it is important to assess the building and the way it is used in order to understand:

- the heritage values (significance) of the building

- the construction and condition of the building fabric and building services

- the existing hygrothermal behaviour of the building

- the likely effectiveness and value for money of measures to improve energy performance

- the impact of the measures on significance

- the technical risks associated with the measures

This will help to identify the measures best suited to an individual building or household, taking behaviour into consideration as well as the building envelope and services

Technical risks

Altering the thermal performance of older buildings is not without risks. The most significant risk is that of creating condensation which can be on the surface of a building component or between layers of the building fabric, which is referred to as 'interstitial condensation'. Condensation can give rise to mould forming and potential health problems for occupants. It can also damage the building fabric through decay. Avoiding the risk of condensation can be complex as a wide range of variables come into play.

Where advice is given in this series of guidance notes on adding insulation into existing permeable construction, we generally consider that insulation which has hygroscopic properties is used as this offers a beneficial 'buffering' effect during fluctuations in temperature and vapour pressure, thus reducing the risk of surface and interstitial condensation occurring. However, high levels of humidity can still pose problems even when the insulation is hygroscopic. Insulation materials with low permeability are not entirely incompatible with older construction but careful thought needs to be given to reducing levels of water vapour moving through such construction either by means of effectively ventilated cavities or through vapour control layers.

The movement of water vapour through parts of the construction is a key issue when considering thermal upgrading, but many other factors need to be considered to arrive at an optimum solution such as heating regimes and the orientation and exposure of the particular building.

More research is needed to help us fully understand the passage of moisture through buildings and how certain forms of construction and materials can mitigate these risks. For older buildings there is no 'one size fits all' solution, each building needs to be considered and an optimum solution devised.

Technical details

The technical drawings included in this guidance document are diagrammatic only and are used to illustrate general principles. They are not intended to be used as drawings for purposes of construction.

Older buildings need to be evaluated individually to assess the most suitable form of construction based on a wide variety of possible variables.

Historic England does not accept liability for loss or damage arising from the use of this information.

1 Pitched Roof Construction and Materials

The pitched roof is the most common roof form used in traditional buildings and roof trusses are almost always made from timber. There are several different types of timber roof construction which vary depending upon the age of the building, its structural form and local traditions.

Metal framed buildings are not discussed in this guidance, other than to note that special care should be taken with the insulation of their roofs because of the increased risk of thermal bridging and condensation.

The common elements of timber pitched roof construction are:

Rafter: An inclined timber in the roof frame of a pitched roof that supports the battens and roof coverings, they are usually one of a pair. In many traditional roofs there are two types of rafters: principal rafters of a large section that carry the main loads of the roof, and intermediate common rafters of smaller section between the principal rafters.

Purlin: A horizontal timber that provides intermediate support to common rafters.

Tie beam: A major horizontal timber that spans between the top of opposite walls and connects a pair of principal rafters.

Collar: A horizontal member connecting rafters at a point between above their feet and below the apex of the roof.

Post: A substantial vertical member, usually a component of the main framework.

Battens: Horizontal timbers of small section fixed to the rafters upon which tiles or slates are laid.

Counter-battens: Timbers of small section fixed at right angles or obliquely to the direction of the battens between them and the surface below.

Sarking board: Boarding provided between the roof coverings and the rafters whose main function is to reduce wind loading but they also act as a secondary barrier against water penetration and can considerably strengthen the roof by stiffening and bracing the rafters. Sarking board is common in Scottish roofs, where the slates or tiles are typically fixed directly to the board. Modern sarking board is typically laid directly onto the rafters and can act as an additional insulation layer.

Warm Roofs and Cold Roofs

In this guidance the term 'cold roof space' or 'cold roof' is used to describe a pitched roof with insulation at the level of the horizontal ceiling of the uppermost floor, leaving an unheated roof space (attic or loft) above the insulation. In contrast a 'warm roof space' or 'warm roof' has insulation between or just under or over the sloping rafters, so that the whole of the volume under the roof can be heated and used. Some buildings have combinations of these two arrangements.

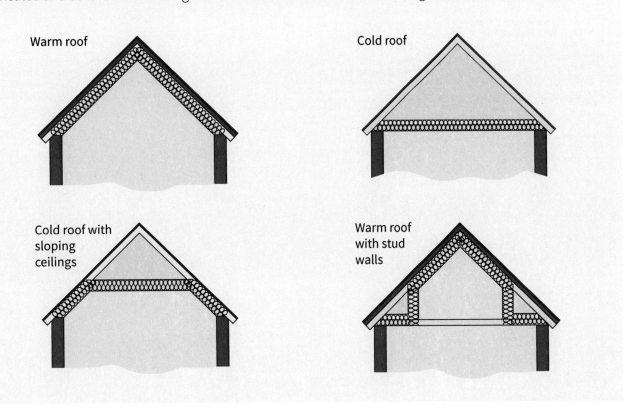

Warm roof

Cold roof

Cold roof with sloping ceilings

Warm roof with stud walls

1.1   Internal finishes to pitched roofs

Most traditional roofs consist solely of tiles or slates laid on battens over the rafters. Internal finishes may be found to the underside of pitched roofs, and because of their scarcity they will need to be given special consideration. Examples of the following may be found:

Torching: Mortar-pointing provided to the underside of tiles and slates. Torching acted as means of reducing wind-blown rain and snow from entering the roof and also helps to hold the coverings in place in strong winds.

Boarded ceilings: Close-boarding is very similar to a sarking-board and was in many cases left exposed to the underside. It can be found in some Georgian buildings and 19th century churches.

Lath and plaster ceilings and partitions: Many roofs were under-drawn with plaster, either lime or earth as they provided accommodation or a space used for storage. In many cases the plaster is contemporary with the construction of the building and is therefore a significant part of its history and should be retained wherever possible. The presence of historic internal finishes such as these on the underside of pitched roofs will mean that insulation at rafter level may not be appropriate or the design of the roof insulation will have to be carefully considered.

1.2 Roof coverings

There are many types of roof covering found on traditional buildings. These reflect the materials that were readily available locally and contribute to the distinctive building vernacular of the area. Not until the Industrial Revolution did mass produced materials, such as Welsh slate or machine made tiles, become common outside the area in which they were found or made.The type of roof material, its form and detailing is usually a significant part of the character of older buildings. This character should not be compromised when making energy efficiency improvements.

Roof coverings are exposed to the worst of the weather and therefore need to be regularly inspected and maintained. Roofs may have been stripped or recovered, especially if they are over a century old. Many of the tiles or slates may still be of historic interest as they may have been reused, so as many as possible should be incorporated into the new roof. Any unusual details should be recorded. However, where a roof appears not to have been stripped and recovered in recent years (usually indicated by the lack of a roofing felt) it would be prudent to determine if any historic fabric of interest survives so that it can be retained, or at least recorded before works commence.

The importance of traditional 'breathing' performance

Most traditional buildings are made of permeable materials and do not incorporate the barriers to external moisture such as cavities, rain-screens, damp-proof courses, vapour barriers and membranes which are standard in modern construction. As a result, the permeable fabric in historic structures tends to absorb more moisture, which is then released by internal and external evaporation. When traditional buildings are working as they were designed to, the evaporation will keep dampness levels in the building fabric below the levels at which decay can start to develop. This is often referred to as a 'breathing' building.

If properly maintained a 'breathing' building has definite advantages over a modern impermeable building. Permeable materials such as lime and/or earth based mortars, renders, plasters and limewash act as a buffer for environmental moisture, absorbing it from the air when humidity is high, and releasing it when the air is dry. Modern construction relies on mechanical extraction to remove water vapour formed by the activities of occupants.

As traditional buildings need to 'breathe' the use of vapour barriers and many materials commonly found in modern buildings must be avoided when making improvements to energy efficiency, as these materials can trap and hold moisture and create problems for the building. The use of modern materials needs to be based upon an informed analysis where the implications of their inclusion and the risk of problems are fully understood.

It is also important that buildings are well maintained, otherwise improvements made in energy efficiency will be cancelled out by the problems associated with water ingress and/ or excessive draughts.

Figure 1
An impervious bitumen felt roof underlay has allowed condensation to form which is staining the roof timbers and causing decay.
© Oxley Conservation.

1.3 Ventilation and breathing performance

Roofs were generally not insulated in the past but the roof spaces were usually well ventilated. Often roof coverings had many small gaps through which wind, but not rain could penetrate. As a consequence roof timbers were well ventilated and close to the outside temperature. The moisture levels in timbers were kept below the range at which decay can begin.

Where insulation is introduced it is important that the traditional 'breathing' performance of older buildings is taken into consideration to avoid creating risks for the building and the occupants.

The presence of impervious roofing felt makes it extremely difficult to successfully install insulation in a roof and can increase the long-term risks to the roof timbers.

Roofing/Sarking felt

Many buildings with sloping roofs covered in tiles or slate have had roofing felt added when they were re-covered in the 20th century. Roofing felt was provided to equalise wind pressure and reduce the risk of tiles or slates being blown off in stormy conditions. It has the secondary benefit of acting as a barrier against water penetration. As a consequence it has reduced the frequency of maintenance and repairs.

Unless the roof was recovered within the last ten years or so it is likely the roofing felt is impervious rather than vapour permeable. Impervious felts have worked well in most situations but can cause problems of condensation (with associated mould growth and timber decay) where there is inadequate ventilation within the roof space. This is particularly likely where large amounts of water vapour are being produced from cooking, bathing and high occupancy levels in the building and this excessive moisture is not ventilated away.

2 Insulating at Rafter Level

The 'warm roof' system is used extensively in new construction and the systems for installing insulation in modern buildings are well understood. However, there are relatively few examples of older buildings that have been insulated at rafter level. This makes it difficult to assess the long-term performance of insulation materials and methods by studying real examples.

Poorly designed insulation can have adverse effects on the performance of the building, the condition of the fabric and the health of the occupants. Considerable planning and attention to detail is required to minimise these risks.

Well-detailed insulation at rafter level can:

- reduce excessive heat loss

- reduce excessive solar gain

- achieve reduced air infiltration

- be compatible with the performance characteristics of older buildings

If a historically significant ceiling or lining is installed on the underside of the rafters which cannot be removed, insulation can only be installed at rafter level by stripping the roof coverings (tiles or slates) and inserting the insulation from above. This is easiest and most economical when a roof is undergoing repair and the roof covering is being stripped. If no works are planned or necessary then insulating at rafter level may not be economic or appropriate.

Warm roofs and cold roofs

In this guidance the term 'cold roof space' or 'cold roof' is used to describe a pitched roof with insulation at the level of the horizontal ceiling of the uppermost floor, leaving an unheated roof space (attic or loft) above the insulation. In contrast a 'warm roof space' or 'warm roof' has insulation between or just under or over the sloping rafters, so that the whole of the volume under the roof can be heated and used. Some buildings have combinations of these two arrangements.

It is very important to achieve good airtight detailing, particularly when placing insulation between rafters or from below (from within the accommodation). Even small gaps in insulation can create problems significantly reducing the benefits of any improvements and creating potential problems of cold-bridging and condensation.

When insulation is installed in a building, extra attention needs to be paid to the risk of condensation. In particular it is important that water vapour is removed at source wherever possible by means of mechanical extractors and/ or ventilation using existing window openings.

2.1 Positioning the insulation

Raising the roof line

One of the most important factors in deciding the method of adding insulation at rafter level will be the acceptability of a raised roof line. The addition of insulating sarking boards and counter battens will require the roof to be raised. The depth will depend on the materials used and whether insulation can be added between the rafters as well. It is likely to be between 75 mm and 100 mm and possibly more depending what depth can be achieved between the rafters.

If the roof within a terrace is raised to accommodate insulation this would break up the ridge- line, creating visual and technical problems. This option would need careful consideration before being implemented. In certain detached historic buildings, such as those with low parapet walls or ornate eaves, raising the roof line could result in an unacceptable change in appearance. Planning and or listed building consents will often be required to raise the roof line.

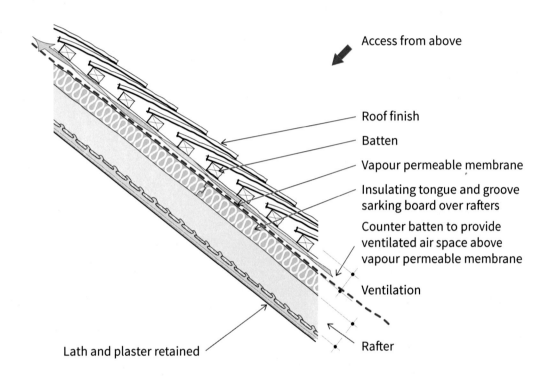

Access from above

Roof finish

Batten

Vapour permeable membrane

Insulating tongue and groove sarking board over rafters

Counter batten to provide ventilated air space above vapour permeable membrane

Ventilation

Rafter

Lath and plaster retained

Figure 2 (above): Insulation above the rafters only
Insulation here is shown only on top of the rafters if it was not considered possible to place insulation between the rafters as well. An air path is provided above the sarking insulation by counter-battening. The use of thicker sarking insulation together with counter-battening could raise the roof by at least 75mm which might pose a number of detailing problems.

Figure 3 (left)
Tongue and grooved wood-fibre board is being used above the rafters as well as sheep's wool insulation between the rafters.
© Oxley Conservation.

Above the rafters

Insulation boards can be added on top of the rafters beneath the battens and roof coverings. This is often referred to as 'sarking' insulation.

Advantages:

- Tight fitting insulation over the rafters reduces air infiltration, improving the performance of the insulation

- Insulation placed over the rafters can be fitted in an unbroken layer, avoiding the risk of thermal bridging where other objects cross the insulation layer

- Insulation above the rafters leaves the structure of the roof on the warm, dry side of the insulation. This reduces the risk of condensation on the timbers, and the timber decay that could follow

- The provision of sarking board with a relatively high density effectively increases the mass of the lightweight construction of the roof. This reduces overheating of the internal environment from solar gain

- The mass of the sarking board will also absorb thermal gains from appliances and occupants internally, improving internal environmental conditions. Nevertheless, ventilation control is critical if unwanted summer gains are to be reduced during the day and removed at night

- Historic lath and plaster ceilings and stud walls can be retained

Figure 4 (left)
Each eaves detail needs careful thought once sarking insulation is added. Often bespoke solutions have to be devised to achieve effective improvement.
© Oxley Conservation.

Figure 5 (right)
Setting out the proposed eaves detail with tiling, counter-battens, and sarking insulation.
© Oxley Conservation.

Disadvantages:

- It is expensive to provide the scaffolding and temporary roofing needed to install sarking boards

- The installation of sarking boards will require the height of the roof to be raised, typically by between 25mm and 100mm. This will in turn require changes to the verges and eaves

- Undulations in the roof slopes and the rafters are often important to the character of the building but they can create difficulties in achieving successful jointing between the sarking boards. This requires great care on site to prevent the benefits of the sarking insulation being negated by gaps at their joints

- High standards of workmanship are needed to achieve effective insulation, careful jointing and sealing of the gaps is essential

- Adding additional weight to the rafters which may already be near or over their limits of span could mean the roof will need to be strengthened

Between the rafters

Alternatively insulation can be added between the rafters.

Advantages:

- Does not require the height of the roof to be visibly increased

- Lower cost.

- Lath and plaster ceilings and stud walls can be retained if the insulation is added from above

Disadvantages:

- Worthwhile improvements in thermal performance will only be achieved if the rafters are deep enough to accommodate a thick layer of insulation

- If there is no sarking insulation the top face of the rafters will be exposed and provide a potential thermal bridge

- A high level of workmanship is required to ensure that gaps between the rafters and the insulation are kept to a minimum. Such gaps can result in air infiltration. Soft pliable insulation materials such as quilt and batts are better in this respect than rigid sheets

- The installation of impermeable insulation between rafters could result in water vapour permeating into rafters and in extreme cases this could rot timbers

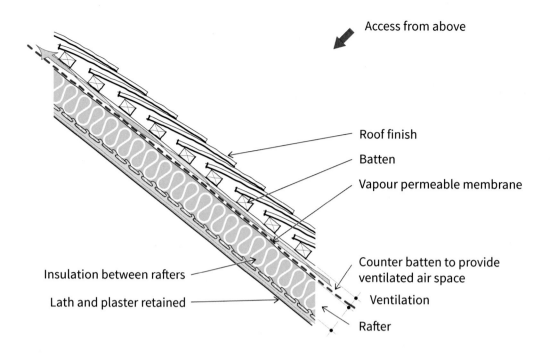

Access from above

Roof finish

Batten

Vapour permeable membrane

Counter batten to provide ventilated air space

Ventilation

Rafter

Insulation between rafters

Lath and plaster retained

Figure 6 (top): Insulation between the rafters only
No sarking insulation is used here so the roof will only be raised by the depth of the counter-battening which provide ventilation space between the insulation and the roof finish.

Figure 7 (bottom left)
Sheep's wool insulation added between rafters.
© Oxley Conservation.

Figure 8 (bottom right)
The use of natural insulation materials can be very beneficial in older buildings due their permeability. Here sheep's wool has been placed between the rafters with reed matting fixed to the underside providing a key for a lime plaster finish.
© Oxley Conservation.

Below the rafters

This can be a good solution where an internal roof-space allows access, although care will be required to ensure suitable ventilation above the insulation to prevent rot in the rafters.

Where historic sloping ceilings exist, but have been previously replaced or are so damaged that they warrant replacement, adding insulation below them to form an insulating ceiling can be considered. An insulating ceiling could also be added beneath an existing ceiling providing it is acceptable to cover that ceiling.

Advantages:

■ Does not require the height of the roof to be visibly increased

■ Could potentially be installed without stripping the roof coverings. This would depend on the type and condition of the roofing felt. If it is an impervious felt stripping of the coverings would be required

■ Allows near continuous installation of insulation with well-sealed gaps

Disadvantages:

■ May change the appearance and proportions of the internal areas affected

■ Cannot achieve significant improvements without potential loss of useable space

■ Difficult to detail at junctions, around openings and where structure penetrates the insulation layer- may result in concealment or loss of historic cornices, frames etc

■ Although existing historic ceilings could be left in place above the insulation, the method is not readily reversible. Future removal may result in extensive damage or the loss of the existing ceilings

■ If the building is listed, the replacement of ceilings will normally require listed building consent. The local planning authority should be consulted prior to the removal of existing ceilings, particularly those that are historically significant

Combined approach

In many applications a combination of methods will be required, the most common being insulation above and between the rafters

Advantages:

■ This is likely to be the most effective method of insulating at rafter level

■ Provides combined advantages of the different approaches and negates many of the disadvantages

Disadvantages:

■ Additional cost

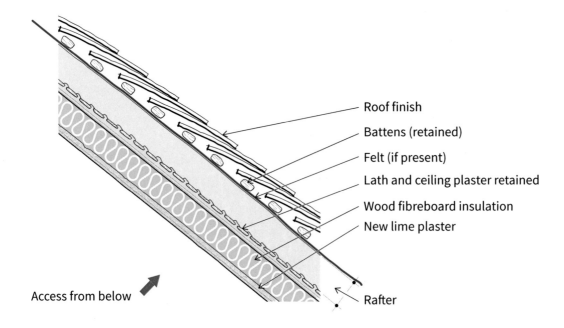

Roof finish

Battens (retained)

Felt (if present)

Lath and ceiling plaster retained

Wood fibreboard insulation

New lime plaster

Access from below

Rafter

Figure 9 (above left)
Wood-fibre insulation has been fitted to the underside of the rafters providing a tight fit which increases its effectiveness. This type of insulation also provides the added benefits of thermal mass and sound insulation. Wood-fibre board is quite inflexible so if the rafters are quite uneven then some levelling will be required.
© Oxley Conservation.

Figure 10 (above right)
Care is needed when fixing insulation around existing roof timbers. Here the joists have been sealed with tape to maintain air-tightness.
© Oxley Conservation.

Figure 11 (bottom): Insulation below the rafters and ceiling (lath and plaster ceiling retained)
Insulation here is added from inside below the existing ceiling finish which is retained in-situ.

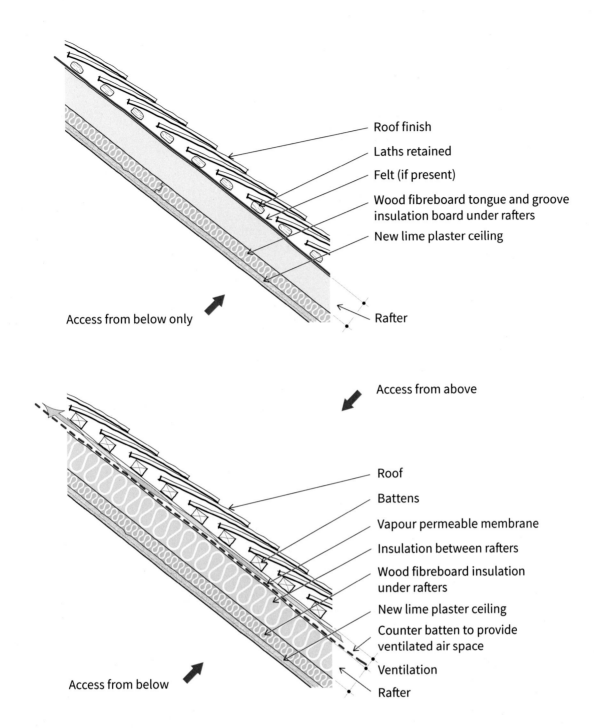

Roof finish

Laths retained

Felt (if present)

Wood fibreboard tongue and groove insulation board under rafters

New lime plaster ceiling

Access from below only

Rafter

Access from above

Roof

Battens

Vapour permeable membrane

Insulation between rafters

Wood fibreboard insulation under rafters

New lime plaster ceiling

Counter batten to provide ventilated air space

Ventilation

Access from below

Rafter

Figure 12 (top): Insulation below the rafters (new lime plaster ceiling)
The existing ceiling is removed and insulation is just added below the rafters. Insulation could be added between the rafters as well providing an air path was provided below the roof finish (50mm is recommended).

Figure 13 (bottom): Insulation between and below the rafters
This proposal requires access from above and below the roof. Rather than add sarking insulation the existing ceiling is removed and insulation is added to the underside of the rafters and between the rafters. If the insulation between the rafters was not to their full depth then an air path could be provided and all the work could be undertaken from below avoiding the need to counter-batten.

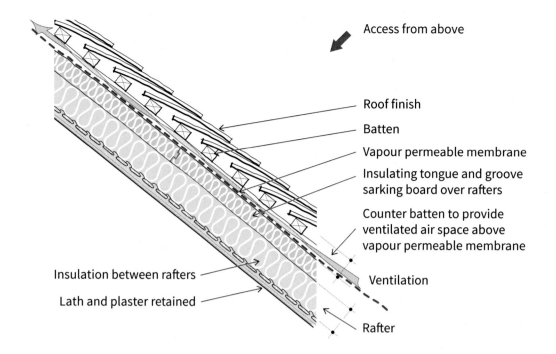

Access from above

Roof finish

Batten

Vapour permeable membrane

Insulating tongue and groove sarking board over rafters

Counter batten to provide ventilated air space above vapour permeable membrane

Ventilation

Rafter

Insulation between rafters

Lath and plaster retained

Figure 14 (top): Insulation used above the rafters
Insulation is shown here placed between the rafters with a thinner layer of sarking insulation placed on top of the rafters which might be a tongued and grooved wood-fibre board. An air path is provided above the sarking insulation by counter-battening below the roof finish.

Figure 15 (bottom)
Roof and wall insulation being combined in a well detailed and compatible system
© Oxley Conservation.

3 Insulation Materials for Roofs

During the last fifteen years 'natural' vapour permeable insulation materials have been developed and introduced into traditional buildings in the course of repairs and improvements. Before this time the insulation materials available were designed for use in modern buildings and so were to an extent incompatible with the performance of traditional buildings.

The presence of dampness in any parts of the fabric of many buildings of traditional construction cannot be ruled out because of their porous nature. Condensation can occur at the surface or even within the pores of vapour permeable materials. Insulation materials added to traditional buildings therefore need to be able to absorb and release moisture and perform well as an insulator within a range of moisture contents.

3.1 Insulation used above the rafters

Insulation added above rafters will typically be a rigid insulating board. The most appropriate material for older buildings is probably wood-fibre board, which has the following performance characteristics:

- Sufficient thermal qualities to reduce heat loss

- Sufficient thermal qualities to reduce the risks of cold bridging above the rafters

- Sufficient thermal mass to reduce the risks of over-heating

- Can be laid to be tight fitting to reduce gaps and unwanted air infiltration. Wood-fibre boards are available with interlocking joints to assist with this

- Vapour permeable; to achieve a 'breathing' construction

- Water-resistant wood-fibre boards are also available which can function as a secondary barrier to rain penetration and a temporary rain shield during installation

Condensation in roofs

All air contains some water vapour, but warm air can hold more water vapour than cold air. When warm, damp air is cooled it will reach a temperature at which it cannot hold all the vapour in it, and the water will condense out. This temperature is called the dew point.

Warm damp air passing over a cold surface will be cooled locally below the dew point and condensation will take place. This effect causes the familiar condensation on the inside of cold windows.

Sections where insulation is missing or ineffective are called 'thermal bridges'. Common thermal bridges in roofs insulated at the rafters include:

- around the rafters, particularly to the top face where there is no sarking insulation above

- joints and gaps between individual sarking insulation boards

- joints and gaps between the sarking insulation and abutting walls, chimneys etc

- around pipes, cables and light fittings that penetrate the roof

In winter thermal bridges will be cold. Warm, moist air passing over a thermal bridge will cause condensation to occur at the bridge. Often this causes spots of mould growth, which are both unsightly and potentially hazardous to health. Condensation forming near structural timbers can be absorbed into the timbers increasing the risk of active timber decay.

The risks to any particular building will be dependent on a number of influencing factors, with perhaps the most significant being the amount of water vapour being produced. The greater the intensity of use the greater the risk of problems will be. The more people there are in the building producing water vapour from breathing, cooking and bathing -particularly the use of showers - the more likely that poor detailing will be exposed and problems suffered, such as thermal bridging and condensation.

Without extensive stripping and re-covering of roofs and the provision of vapour permeable roofing felts there will be a continued risk of condensation damp and associated defects. Impervious felts should be replaced when roofing works are being carried out.

3.2 Insulation used between the rafters

There are several types of materials suitable for insulation between the rafters. The most appropriate materials are natural-fibre based insulation such as sheep's wool or hemp-fibre. These have the following performance characteristics:

■ They are hygroscopic; that is, they can absorb but also release excess moisture

■ They retain their thermal qualities when damp

■ They are non-hazardous fibres

The use of flexible insulation batts and rolls between the rafters improves the ability to achieve a tight-fitting insulation. In contrast, rigid insulation boards can be difficult to cut and scribe tightly between rafters, which in many cases are highly irregular.

Cellulose insulation (fibres derived from newsprint) is an alternative material, but its performance can be compromised if it comes into contact with moisture. Loose-fill cellulose insulation is unsuitable for use between pitched rafters because of its tendency to settle. Such settlement would leave a gap near the ridge where a cold bridge can develop

3.3 Insulation used beneath the rafters

The most appropriate materials for use beneath the rafters are wood-fibre boards with a breathable lime plaster.

3.4 Inappropriate materials and methods

Durability
In selecting the most appropriate insulation material for each building it is important to ensure that the material will continue to perform for many years. If the material is likely to settle then allowance should be made for that. If the insulation is likely to suffer physical degradation, a more robust material would be appropriate. Similarly, insulation which tolerates vapour movement will be required if high moisture levels are anticipated nearby.

Vapour barriers
Whilst the installation of vapour barriers to control condensation within insulation and associated structures is theoretically effective, it is in reality very difficult to install them in historic buildings. Particular difficulties occur in the following situations:

■ Where the insulated roof slope abuts permeable construction, such as timber, brick or stonework. The vapour barrier will be easily by-passed causing increased condensation and potential damage

■ Where it is necessary to seal a vapour barrier around an existing opening such as a rooflight or an access hatch

■ Where there is a risk the vapour barrier may be punctured in use. Where punctures occur, condensation and consequent damage will normally occur within the historic construction this exposes

Due to these difficulties it is preferable within historic buildings to use vapour permeable insulation and ancillary construction which avoids concentrations of moisture and allows the condensation that inevitably does occur to evaporate away as quickly as possible.

Figure 16
Sheep's wool insulation with a vapour permeable
membrane added close to the eaves.
© Oxley Conservation

Foils and foil faced materials

A range of modern insulation materials use
reflective foils to try to reduce heat loss further
and claim to either substitute for insulation or to
increase its effectiveness. These appear to allow
useful performance with thinner materials. Their
performance can in reality often be much less
than is claimed and the foils themselves introduce
all the disadvantages of vapour barriers.

Sprayed foam insulation

Another type of insulation currently available is
spray applied insulating foam to the underside of
roofs. This type of application can have several
disadvantages for traditional buildings:

- It is a short-term solution that will last only
  until the roof coverings need to be renewed
  or re-laid

- It can prejudice the future repair and re-use
  of existing coverings because treated tiles,
  slates cannot be reused

- It could increase the risk of decay to battens
  where the foam is applied directly to the
  underside of the coverings

- Any damage to the coverings could allow
  water to penetrate into the foam

4 Amount of Insulation

The Approved Document that accompanies Part L of the Building Regulations for existing dwellings (ADL1B 2010) calls for insulation between the rafters of a pitched roof to have a U-value of 0.18 W/m2K. Such levels of insulation are quite high, but are potentially achievable in ways that are not harmful to historic buildings.

U-values

U-values measure how quickly energy will pass through one square metre of a barrier when the air temperatures on either side differ by one degree.

U-values are expressed in units of Watts per square metre per degree of temperature difference (W/m2K).]

One of the benefits of insulating at rafter level is that insulation can be provided both above and between the rafters. These can combine to achieve relatively high performance standards.

The extent and type of insulation that can be provided between the rafters will be dictated by the size of the rafters, which can vary considerably from slender timbers as little as 75 mm deep to those that are 225 mm deep or more. Obviously, the greater the depth of the rafters the more opportunity there is to provide insulation thereby reducing the amount of insulation required above the rafters and consequently the height the roof needs to be raised. However, it will be difficult for many older buildings to achieve a U-value of 0.18 W/m2K if there are constraints on the thickness of insulation that can be provided above the rafters. For example, to reach a U value of 0.18 W/m2K in a roof with a non-insulating ceiling and 150 mm of insulation between rafters requires an insulating sarking board of about 70 mm thickness.

Part L of the Building Regulations allows for exemptions and special considerations for historic buildings which enables Building Control Officers or Approved Inspectors to take a pragmatic view in order to conserve the appearance and character of the building and avoid technical risks.

5 Installation Checklist

Roofs in traditional buildings are often complex, frequently compounded by a series of additions and alterations. It therefore makes good sense to plan the installation of insulation carefully before starting any work

Consider the following questions and if possible sketch out a roof plan which will help identify the difficult areas:

■ Has the roof been checked for the presence of bats or nesting birds? It is important that roofs are checked before works are programmed as the presence of protected species can cause delays

■ Has the roof been checked for the presence of asbestos? Discovering asbestos insulation or pipe lagging during works could lead to health risks, delays and increased costs

■ Are the insulation materials selected appropriate for buildings with permeable construction?

■ Has the installation of the materials selected been researched so that they can be successfully installed? Different materials will require different design details

■ Has the weight of the insulation materials and associated additions such as counter-battens been considered? Heavier insulation sometimes has an advantage of increased thermal mass but can significantly increase the loading on a roof structure. If in doubt have a structural appraisal of the roof structure carried out

■ Have difficult to detail areas, such as open eaves and verges to gables been fully considered and detailed?

■ Has a strategy for filling gaps and sealing joints been devised?

■ Are all sections of the building's roof to be insulated at rafter level? Designing the junctions between sections insulated at rafter level and sections insulated at ceiling level is both difficult and critical

■ Has the significance of the roof coverings and associated features been assessed before commencement of the works?

■ Has air-pressure testing being considered to assess the effectiveness and performance of the improvements?

■ Consider any wiring that runs up the rafters. It will be difficult to access once the roof is insulated. Cable runs, sockets and recessed light fittings within the insulation are to be avoided. If services need to run over the ceiling they should use conduits attached to the room side of the insulation

■ Has the local authority's conservation officer been consulted with regard to the stripping and recovering of the roof with changed detailing? Consent is likely to be required if the building is listed and will need to be obtained prior to commencement of works

Figure 17
The need for roof repairs provided a cost effective opportunity to add insulation to this Grade I listed building.
© Oxley Conservation

- Is the information about the insulation materials readily available to the contractor and the workforce? Some of the materials may be new to many roofing contractors

- Has the contractor understood the importance of good detailing? The effectiveness of the insulation can be seriously undermined by poor installation at junctions such as eaves and chimneys

5.1 Strip the roof coverings carefully

Existing roof coverings and sarking felt (if present) should be removed carefully. A temporary roof will normally be required to keep out the rain during the works. It is also important to consider the possible effects of unusual wind and structural loading on the roof during removal of the coverings, particularly if the coverings are removed asymmetrically. Coverings suitable for re-use should be put to one side. If the building is particularly old and significant, recording maybe required during the works as a condition of any consent.

Roof spaces should be cleared of debris, dust and dirt with great care so as not to damage historic fabric, such as lath and plaster ceilings and partitions and, in older buildings, wattle and daub panels. Once the roof coverings are removed the constructional detailing and condition of areas previously concealed can be evaluated. This also provides the opportunity to record the exposed roof construction. It might be fifty years at least before the roof coverings are removed again. Recording can include sketches and photographs.

5.2 Removing existing insulation

Any existing loft insulation at ceiling level should be removed so that insulation is concentrated at rafter level. It is unlikely that any existing insulation will be found between the rafters. If any is found it should be removed. The cost of insulation materials is relatively low compared to removing the roof coverings so that when the roof coverings are removed it makes sense to renew the insulation. Great care should be taken when removing old insulation. Protective clothing and dust masks should be worn at all times.

5.3 Repairing and consolidating existing ceilings and partitions

Exposing the top of the rafters gives the opportunity to inspect the top side of any plaster finishes and carry out any repair and consolidation. The repair and consolidation of plaster finishes will assist in removing gaps and cracks where air infiltration will occur. This is very important to the overall effectiveness of the insulation.

If the replacement of existing ceilings is justified an insulated ceiling may be sensible. This will have the benefit of increasing the level of thermal insulation.

Where sloping ceilings are to be replaced, or where new sloping ceilings are to be installed, this work needs to be carried out first. The insulation between the rafters can then be installed resting on the ceilings.

5.4 Installing insulation between the rafters

Install the insulation between the rafters and any vertical walls very carefully. It is important that the insulation fits tightly.

Gaps in the insulation and adjoining building elements, such as the rafters, can allow draughts that reduce the thermal benefits of the insulation, whilst also causing cold spots (thermal bridges) prone to damp and mould growth.

5.5   Installing insulating sarking board

Install the sarking board in accordance with the manufacturer's recommendations

- Sarking boards must be tight-fitting. The use of boards with interlocking tongue and groove joints will assist in improving air-tightness

- The detailing is important so that the insulation will be effective. Sealants, tapes and where appropriate, lapped vapour permeable roofing felt secured with counter battens should be used

Particular attention is required in the following areas:

- joints between two pieces of sarking board at roof junctions (ridges, valleys and hips)

- joints between sarking board and other building elements (chimneys, parapets, gables)

- termination of sarking board at eaves and verges, and around openings, such as rooflights and dormers, that penetrate the sarking board

- If there is doubt about air-tightness a breathable membrane carefully taped at its joints can be installed

Pipes and ducts that pass through the roof construction and vent to the outside are at risk of attracting condensation. The water vapour in the warm moist air from the insulated accommodation passing through these cold, un-insulated pipes and ducts is likely to condense on their inner surfaces. It is important that the design of these ducts takes this into account.

Insulation needs to be physically separated from damp chimneys and gables, party and parapet walls. The thermal performance of insulation that is damp will be significantly reduced, and timbers will also be at risk of being subjected to prolonged dampness and associated decay. Physically separating the insulation from damp chimneys and walls will help to keep the insulation dry.

6 Where to Get Advice

This guidance forms part of a series of thirteen documents which are listed below, providing advice on the principles, risks, materials and methods for improving the energy efficiency of various building elements such as roofs, walls and floors in older buildings.

This series forms part of a wider comprehensive suite of guidance providing good practice advice on adaptation to reduce energy use and the application and likely impact of carbon legislation on older buildings.

The complete series of guidance is available to download from the Historic England website: HistoricEngland.org.uk/energyefficiency

Roofs
- Insulating pitched roofs at rafter level
- Insulating pitched roofs at ceiling level
- Insulating flat roofs
- Insulating thatched roofs
- Open fires, chimneys and flues
- Insulating dormer windows

Walls
- Insulating timber-framed walls
- Insulating solid walls
- Insulating early cavity walls

Windows And Doors
- Draught-proofing windows and doors
- Secondary glazing for windows

Floors
- Insulating suspended timber floors
- Insulating solid ground floors

For information on consents and regulations for energy improvement work see HistoricEngland.org.uk/advice/your-home/saving-energy/consent-regulations

6.1   Contact Historic England

East Midlands
2nd Floor, Windsor House
Cliftonville
Northampton NN1 5BE
Tel: 01604 735460
Email: eastmidlands@HistoricEngland.org.uk

East of England
Brooklands
24 Brooklands Avenue
Cambridge CB2 8BU
Tel: 01223 582749
Email: eastofengland@HistoricEngland.org.uk

Fort Cumberland
Fort Cumberland Road
Eastney
Portsmouth PO4 9LD
Tel: 023 9285 6704
Email: fort.cumberland@HistoricEngland.org.uk

London
1 Waterhouse Square
138-142 Holborn
London EC1N 2ST
Tel: 020 7973 3700
Email: london@HistoricEngland.org.uk

North East
Bessie Surtees House
41-44 Sandhill
Newcastle Upon Tyne NE1 3JF
Tel: 0191 269 1255
Email: northeast@HistoricEngland.org.uk

North West
3rd Floor, Canada House
3 Chepstow Street
Manchester M1 5FW
Tel: 0161 242 1416
Email: northwest@HistoricEngland.org.uk

South East
Eastgate Court
195-205 High Street
Guildford GU1 3EH
Tel: 01483 252020
Email: southeast@HistoricEngland.org.uk

South West
29 Queen Square
Bristol BS1 4ND
Tel: 0117 975 1308
Email: southwest@HistoricEngland.org.uk

Swindon
The Engine House
Fire Fly Avenue
Swindon SN2 2EH
Tel: 01793 445050
Email: swindon@HistoricEngland.org.uk

West Midlands
The Axis
10 Holliday Street
Birmingham B1 1TF
Tel: 0121 625 6870
Email: westmidlands@HistoricEngland.org.uk

Yorkshire
37 Tanner Row
York YO1 6WP
Tel: 01904 601948
Email: yorkshire@HistoricEngland.org.uk